BREEZEWOOD, PA
AUG 9
—AM
1965
15533

Post Card

GREYHOUND in POSTCARDS
Buses, Depots and Post Houses

From the collection of John Dockendorf

Dylan Frautschi, Editor

Iconografix

Iconografix
PO Box 446
Hudson, Wisconsin 54016 USA

Library of Congress Control Number: 2004102901

ISBN 1-58388-130-1

04 05 06 07 08 09 6 5 4 3 2 1

Printed in China

Cover and book design by Dan Perry

BOOK PROPOSALS

Iconografix is a publishing company specializing in books for transportation enthusiasts. We publish in a number of different areas, including Automobiles, Auto Racing, Buses, Construction Equipment, Emergency Equipment, Farming Equipment, Railroads & Trucks. The Iconografix imprint is constantly growing and expanding into new subject areas.

Authors, editors, and knowledgeable enthusiasts in the field of transportation history are invited to contact the Editorial Department at Iconografix, Inc., PO Box 446, Hudson, WI 54016.

Introduction

As part of Greyhound's objective to establish the nation's largest national intercity bus system, the company began an aggressive campaign to build its own terminals in the 1930s. Most of these facilities were of art deco style with blue-glazed tile, rounded corners and a lighted neon sign with at least the company's name, and often its "running dog" logo. At the same time, to better serve the traveling public, Greyhound began building a network of over one-hundred restaurants and rest stops, commonly called post houses. To advertise and promote these facilities, these depots and post houses were featured on commercial postcards available for riders to send home messages while they were traveling. An interesting cross-section of many of the Greyhound depot restaurant and rest stop postcards are featured in this publication to provide the reader a visual picture of the Company's vast nationwide network of these facilities.

The historical Greyhound-related postcards represented here include a mix of early black and white, "real photo" postcards that were popular before World War II; colorful "linen" postcards that were introduced in the 1930s, which were very popular until the early 1950s; and "photochrome" color postcards that have been popular from the 1950s until today. Most of these postcards are at least twenty-five years old and many are much older. Also, a number of the pictured postcards are very rare. Therefore, this publication provides the reader a unique opportunity to see some Greyhound facilities that they may have never seen before and may be unaware even existed.

It is hoped that seeing these wonderful Greyhound depots and post houses will bring back to readers fond memories of their past travel experiences. Also, hopefully it will bring a greater appreciation to readers, not previously familiar with these facilities, a greater appreciation of the wonderful network of Greyhound depots, restaurants and rest stops that used to exist before automotive and airline travel became so popular. Enjoy your journey!

John Dockendorf
February, 2004

About the John Dockendorf Collection

John Dockendorf has been an avid collector of paper, and non-paper bus memorabilia for over twenty-five years. His extensive collection of bus postcards, match covers, and toy and model buses is one of the largest in the nation, and among the largest in the world. John is especially proud of his premier collection of North American bus postcards, and welcomes this opportunity to share his unique collection with others who otherwise may not have had an opportunity to see this material before.

Mr. Dockendorf currently serves on the Board of Directors for the Museum of Bus Transportation, which is located in Hershey, Pennsylvania. He is now the Museum's First Vice President and Secretary, also was one of the organization's original six co-founders in 1995. His recent Museum publication, "A Dream Come True" is well known in the bus industry as is his impressive collection of toy and model buses, and bus artifacts, currently on display at the Museum.

John began collecting bus postcards in the late 1980s at the advice of his friend and mentor, Mr. Charles Wotring, of Royal Coach in Mechanicsburg, Pennsylvania. It is to "Charlie" that this book is dedicated, as without his help and support, this publication would not have been possible.

Contents

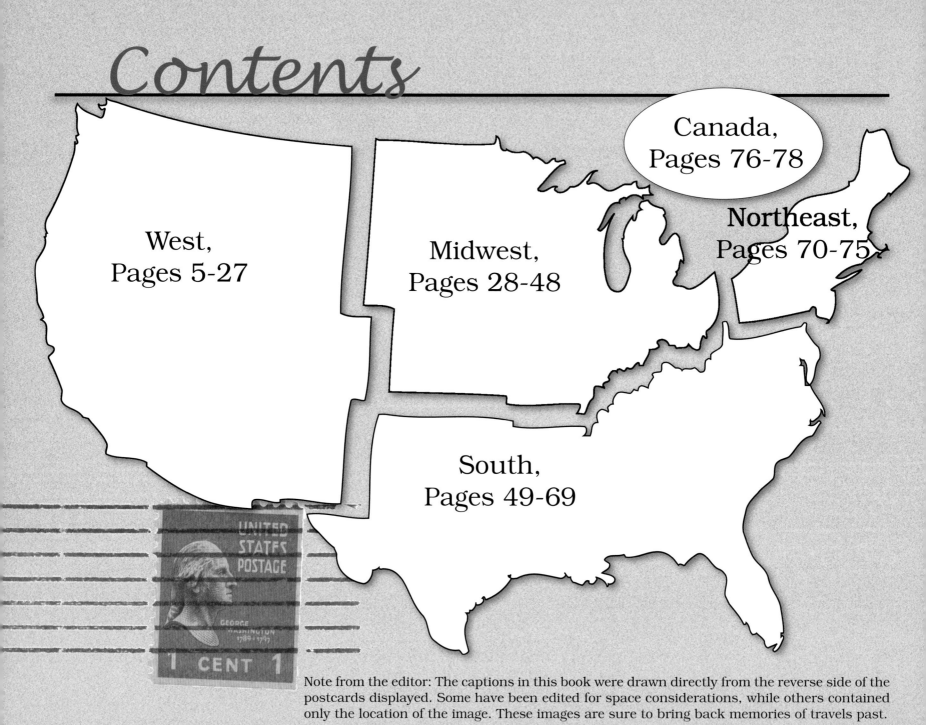

UNITED STATES POSTAGE

GEORGE WASHINGTON 1789-1797

1 CENT 1

Note from the editor: The captions in this book were drawn directly from the reverse side of the postcards displayed. Some have been edited for space considerations, while others contained only the location of the image. These images are sure to bring back memories of travels past.

Greyhound Bus Terminal, Los Angeles, California. America's most modern bus terminal located at Sixth and Los Angeles Streets is comprised of three levels with huge arrival and departure concourses.

Greetings from Riverside, California.

Lynwood, California. Built in 1917, this old Pacific Electric Station is a familiar landmark. The rail line through Lynwood was constructed in 1905.

Greyhound Bus Station, Sacramento, California. From this new, modern station, busses come and go on frequent schedules around the clock.

Banning, California.

Modesto, California.

Indio, California.

Pasadena, California.

Orland, California.

Tracy, California.

Redding, California.

Truckee, California.

The Pickwick Hotel. Broadway at First Avenue, San Diego, California.

Lane's Redwood Flat, California. A popular resort located in a giant redwood forest near the Eel River on U.S 101, 190 miles north of San Francisco.

Little Lake, California. Little lake (3,172 ft. alt.) is located at the lower end of the Alabama Hills and on Highway 395. A few miles north of this tourist settlement is located Owens Lake, some 17 miles long and 10 miles wide, named for Richard Owen, a member of John C. Fremont's 1845 expedition.

Pixely, California. Between Bakersfield and Los Angeles on wide U.S. Highway 99 is this stopping point for the Greyhound Busses and motorists. Excellent food, refreshments, and all accommodations for the traveler.

Greyhound Bus Depot Santa Rosa, California. Complete facilities for the traveler at this new, modern bus station include a large, comfortable waiting room, News Stand, and Restaurant. Gateway to the Redwood Empire and Russian River Resorts, Santa Rosa is efficiently served by this popular means of transportation.

Barstow, California. Thousands of vacation-bound travelers enjoy their stops at the Greyhound Post Houses. These are located at convenient intervals across the United States and Canada. Here is to be found fine food and drinks along with interesting gift shops. The traveler enjoys the luxurious duel-level air-conditioned buses that take one to hundreds of areas in America.

Greyhound Bus Station, Fresno, California. Greyhound Post Cafeteria. Main Dining Room has seating capacity for 210 people, plus special Banquet Room accommodating 60 guests.

Tip Top Café in Blythe, California. A good place to eat.

San Luis Obispo, California.

San Luis Obispo, California.

Clearlake Highlands, California.

Baxter, California.

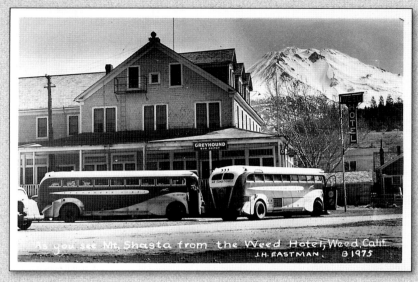

Weed, California.

Ukiah, California.

Victorville, California.

Colfax, California.

11

Desert Center, California. Dedicated to the service of humanity in mid-desert. Desert Center was founded by Stephen A (Desert Steve) Ragsdale in 1921. Its main street is 100 miles long.

Greyhound Bus Depot, Bakersfield, California. This Greyhound Bus Terminal and Posthouse Cafeteria was completed in 1961. It is a most modern facility in every respect and adds to the beauty of downtown Bakersfield.

Greetings from Vallejo, California

Vallejo, California. Founded-1851. This was California's state capital in 1852 for about one week, and again a year later, for just over one month. Despite the departure of the legislature in 1853, the town prospered, for that same year the United States purchased Mare Island for a Navy Yard.

Greyhound Bus Depot, 105-3rd Ave, Yuma, Arizona.

Flagstaff, Arizona. From this depot visitors embark for the Grand Canyon, Monument Valley, Oak Creek Canyon, and other world-famous scenic wonders.

Martin's Cafeteria, Gila Bend, Arizona. U.S. Highway 80 Delicious food-Novelties-curios. A must for southwestern desert travelers. Agent Pacific Greyhound Lines.

Greyhound Bus Terminal, First Street and East Van Buren, Phoenix, Arizona. Completed at a cost of over one million dollars, this new bus terminal is one of the finest in America.

Automat Cafeteria 168 Navajo Blvd. Holbrook, Arizona. First eating establishment of this kind in Arizona.

Chico, California.

San Francisco, California.

Crescent City, California.

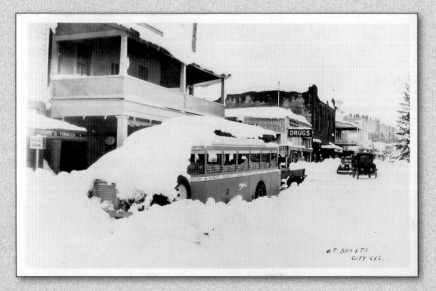

Mt. Shasta City, California.

Salome, Arizona.

Benson, Arizona.

Ash Fork, Arizona.

Dateland, Arizona.

Tucson, Arizona. Grey Chef Restaurant and Cafeteria. "Just good food and 24 hr. service". Corner of Broadway and Church St.

Desert View Trading Post on Yarnell Hill near Yarnell, Arizona. This beautiful spot is a welcome stop for travelers coming out of the Valley of the sun on U.S. Highway 89. The immaculate air-conditioned rooms are filled with fine gifts and hard to find items like Sassafras tea and candy, Old Country smoked hams and cheeses.

Salt Lake City, Utah. Greyhound Terminal Building, Salt Lake City. This is one of the finest bus stations in the country. It accommodates two hundred arriving and departing schedules daily of the Greyhound Lines, Bamberger, Salt Lake & Tooele Stages, Salt Lake & Coalville Stages, and Lewis Bros. Stages. The running dog on the corner sign measures 26 feet in length and is one of the largest in the country.

Long a favorite among tourists, central Utah's finest restaurant, Café Ilene, has operated in its present location since 1922—a period of 30 years. Located at Fillmore, Utah, on U.S. 91, this new and modern $70,000 bus stop restaurant with 24-hour service is owned and operated by John and Ilene Cooper.

St. George, Utah. The Big Hand, one of Southern Utah's most popular eating places. St. George is a picturesque community at the gateway to Utah's National Parks and was founded in 1861 by the Cotton Mission and the area is still known as Utah's Dixie.

Stateline Service Wendover. (on the Nevada, Utah line.) Routes 40 and 50. Hotel, Coffee shop, Bar, Casino, The State Room Cocktail Lounge and Dining Room, Motel, Service Station, and garage. Air-conditioned, steam heated. Open 24-hours. Home of the giant cowboy "Wendover Will" 64 feet tall, weight 9 tons. Largest mechanical cowboy sign in the world. Enjoy the spot where the West begins.

Bus Depot, Roswell, New Mexico.

O'dell Cafeteria and Greyhound Bus Depot. Delicious food-tickets to all points, 108 North Platinum, Deming, New Mexico.

Logan, Utah.

Wickensburg, Arizona.

Deming, New Mexico.

Safford, Arizona.

Tombstone, Arizona.

Painted Desert Park, Arizona.

The Greyhound Station, Globe, Arizona. Is located in the Pinal Mountains with various altitudes obtainable in short distances up to 7,500 feet. Greyhound and White Mountain Passenger Lines leave the station daily. Open 24 hours a day.

Florence Junction, Arizona.

Lake Tahoe, Nevada.

Greyhound Post House and Depot. Las Vegas, Nevada. This beautiful new Post House and Terminal is a very popular meeting place for western tourists. Las Vegas is the crossroads of the West and passengers can make connections here for almost any city in the U.S.A.

Reno, Nevada.

Lovelock, Nevada.

Glendale, Nevada.

Battle Mountain, Nevada.

Elko, Nevada.

Eugene, Oregon.

Portland, Oregon.

Newport, Oregon.

Roseburg, Oregon.

Pendleton, Oregon.

Medford, Oregon.

Klamath Falls, Oregon.

Coos Bay, Oregon.

Richland, Washington.

Colfax Hotel. In the heart of the Paloue County, Colfax, Washington.

Pacific Avenue, Tacoma, Washington. This new million dollar Greyhound Bus terminal is one of the most modern facilities in the United States and serves all points in the area.

Summit Inn, Snoqualmie Pass U.S. Highway 10, Washington. A door that never closes greets travelers around the clock and around the calendar summer and winter at the Summit Inn as they cross this all-weather main cross-state mountain pass highway. A short drive from Seattle, here is located one of the world's finest ski facilities and the most beautiful winter playground areas.

Greyhound Bus Depot, Spokane, Washington. Every convenience for the traveler.

Moses Lake, Washington.

Greyhound Bus Depot. Cheyenne, Wyoming. Being located on trans-continental Highway U.S. 30, the city of Cheyenne has a tremendous amount of travelers coming through, from coast to coast. Travel is also heavy to the south, as well as northern points.

Billings, Montana. This beautiful modern Bus Terminal, one of the finest in the northwest, is located in the business district of the city and serves to link the East with West.

McGaffick Husky Service, Helena, Montana. Truck stop - 24 hour service, Junction U.S.10 & U.S. 91.

Ellensburg, Washington.

Chehalis, Washington.

Yakima, Washington.

Wentatchee, Washington.

Boise, Idaho.

Big Timber, Montana.

Lamar, Colorado.

Babcock's Cafe, Arriba, Colorado. On U. S. Highway 24. Greyhound Bus Depot.

Arriba, Colorado.

N P Avenue, Looking West, showing Greyhound Bus Station, Fargo, N. D.

Fargo, North Dakota.

Stan's Café Air conditioned Greyhound Bus Depot. Grafton, North Dakota.

OVERLAND GREYHOUND BUS DEPOT, SIDNEY, NEBRASKA

Overland Greyhound Bus Depot and Café is located on U.S. Highway 30 in Sidney, Nebraska. Very good food, air-conditioned.

Omaha, Nebraska. Overland Greyhound Bus Depot. One of the finest and most modern bus depots in the Midwest "at the crossroads of the Nation."

Interior View of Greyhound Union Bus Depot.
18th and Farnam Streets. Omaha. Nebraska

LUNCH ROOM FOUNTAIN

M67—Greyhound Bus Depot, Minneapolis, Minn.

NORTHLAND GREYHOUND

City of Lakes and Parks   7A-H2100

Omaha, Nebraska. Interior view of the handsome Greyhound Union Bus Depot, at 18th and Farnam Streets. Fully air-conditioned (even the booths!) and with every feature for comfort and convenience. This ultra-modern terminal is one of the countries finest.

Minneapolis, Minnesota, Greyhound Bus Depot. This new and modern Bus Depot is the terminal point daily for thousands of people traveling to and from all sections of the United States.

Greystone Hotel, Greyhound Bus Depot, Detroit Lakes, Minnesota.

Greyhound Bus Stop, Cambridge Junction, Minnesota. Where good friends meet. Intersection U.S. 12 and M-50 fine food.

Jamestown, North Dakota.

Deerwood, Minnesota.

Brainerd, Minnesota.

Pequot Lakes, Minnesota.

Hinckley, Minnesota.

Hinckley, Minnesota.

Tofte, Minnesota.

Winnebago, Minnesota.

Wisconsin Dells, Wisconsin

Wisconsin Dells, Wisconsin. The Port House. On I.H. 90-94 in scenic Wisconsin Dells is this new Interstate Highway Post House. The distinctive red-roofed cafeteria seats 128 persons, serving travelers, vacationers, local residents and Greyhound bus passengers. The Dells area is noted for scenic boat trips and Indian pageantry.

Brule, Wisconsin. Greyhound Bus Depot. Twin Gables Motel & Café. On the famous Brule River on Highway 2 & 27.

The new Greyhound Bus Depot on 7th between W. Wisconsin & W. Michigan Avenues, Milwaukee, Wisconsin.

Union Bus Depot, Marshalltown, Iowa

Marshalltown, Iowa.

Chicago, Illinois. New Greyhound Terminal. Located at Lake Clark and Randolph Streets. World's largest independently-owned bus terminal. 66,000 square feet of floor space on five levels. Built at a cost of $10,000,000.

Chicago, Illinois.

Greyhound Post House. Gilman, Illinois. "City of the crossroads." Located at the intersection of U.S. Highways 24, 45, 54, this up-to-date and air-conditioned Restaurant serves excellent food to the traveler. Open 24 hours a day - every day of the year.

Pontiac, Illinois.

33

Effingham, Illinois.

Eau Claire, Wisconsin.

Ames, Iowa.

Grinnell, Iowa.

Kalamazoo, Michigan.

Detroit, Michigan.

Wayne, Michigan.

Irish Hills, Michigan.

Greyhound Bus Terminal, Detroit, Mich.

Greyhound Bus Terminal
Grand Rapids, Michigan

Detroit, Michigan. This Greyhound Terminal is a streamlined modern building located in the heart of downtown Detroit at Washington Blvd. and Grand River Ave. It houses the Greyhound, Blue Goose, Eastern Michigan, Canadian Greyhound, Chicago, Cincinnati, Louisville, and the Red Star Way Lines.

Grand Rapids, Michigan.

Irish Hills Hotel — U. S. 112 — Irish Hills District, Michigan

Irish Hills, Michigan.

LANSING, MICHIGAN

Greyhound Bus Station & Cafeteria. Lansing, Michigan.

Greyhound Bus Depot. Saginaw, Michigan.

Greyhound Bus Terminal, Dayton, Ohio

OB-H1557

Dayton, Ohio.

Niles, Michigan. Coach House. Niles, Michigan. 24 hour cafeteria service-catering to the traveling public.

GREYHOUND BUS STATION, CONNEAUT, OHIO

4A432

Conneaut, Ohio.

Greyhound Post House. Mackinaw City, Michigan. Popular Gateway to Michigan's Upper Peninsula. Here you can board a speedy cruiser for an interesting trip to romantic and historical Mackinac Island.

From Mackinaw City, Greyhound buses are ferried across the Straits of Mackinaw to St. Ignace, Michigan.

Half Hour Stop for all Greyhound Busses, Oakwood Tavern, Klinger Lake, Mich. 34209-8

Klinger Lake, Michigan.

Standish, Michigan.

Prudenville, Michigan.

Buckley, Michigan.

Muskegon, Michigan.

Fremont, Ohio.

Greyhound Bus Terminal, Akron, Ohio

STIVAS STUDIO PHOTO

OC-H649

Akron, Ohio. Built at approximate cost of $600,000 the Akron Greyhound Terminal affords all modern conveniences. Fourteen buses may be docked here simultaneously.

23—Greyhound Bus Terminal, Cincinnati, Ohio

2B-H1011

Cincinnati, Ohio.

Greyhound Bus Depot, Portsmouth, Ohio

2B-H1295

Portsmouth, Ohio.

Greyhound Bus Depot and Wayne Theatre, Wooster, Ohio

WAYNE
OLIVIA DE HAVILLAND
ROBERT CUMMINGS
"PRINCESS O'ROURKE"

4B107-N

Wooster, Ohio.

40

Toledo, Ohio.

Greyhound Bus terminal. 111 East Town Street. Columbus, Ohio. Dedicated in 1969, this 2.5 million dollar facility features the most modern comforts for the traveler, including the Post House restaurant, a gift shop, cocktail lounge and is the only one of its kind with a landscaped pedestrian mall.

Cleveland, Ohio. The beautiful new Greyhound Bus Terminal is the largest in the world. Twenty-one loading platforms busy 24 hours a day provide fast bus service to all 48 states, Canada and Mexico. More than 300 people can be seated in the extra-spacious curve-lined lobby. This luxurious bus terminal cost over $1,250,000 to build, serves over 3,000,000 people each year.

Massillon, Ohio. Located at 118 Tremont Avenue, S.E. fringing Massillon's beautiful City Park, it is the finest Bus Terminal for this size city in the country.

Cleveland, Ohio.

Lima, Ohio. Greyhound Post House. Lima, Ohio. For fine food stop at a Greyhound Post House.

South Bend, Indiana. New Greyhound Bus Terminal.

Angola, Indiana.

Rolling Prairie, Indiana.

Kentland, Indiana. Greyhound Post House Cafeteria, known for wonderful food, is open 24 hours a day. Located at intersection of U.S. Highways 41-52 and 24.

Shoals, Indiana.

Valparaiso, Indiana.

Kentland, Indiana.

Evansville, Indiana. Completed in 1938 at a cost of $150,000. One of the most modern bus stations in the United States. 106 buses are scheduled in and out of the station every day.

Barboul's Restaurant. Greyhound Post House. Valparaiso, Indiana. On route 30 and 49. 50 miles from Chicago, if you want a nice steak dinner you will be served well and enjoy a good meal in pleasant surroundings. Special parties and banquets accommodated.

Indianapolis, Indiana.

Jefferson Street, Fort Wayne, Indiana.

Greetings from
KANSAS CITY, MO.

Greyhound Bus Terminal and Post House, 12th & Holmes, Kansas City, Missouri. This is the most modern facility in the country catering to the needs of the bus traveler. The Post House includes a cafeteria, snack bar, cocktail bar, and gift court.

Greyhound Post Terminal, Saint Louis, Missouri.

GREYHOUND BUS TERMINAL—BROADWAY AND DELMAR—ST. LOUIS, MO.

Greyhound Bus Terminal, St. Louis, Missouri. 120 busses pass through this terminal daily. Station complete with news stand, lunch room, barber shop, and large waiting room.

45

Booneville, Missouri.

Booneville, Missouri.

Kingdom City, Missouri.

Lebanon, Missouri.

46

Odessa, Missouri.

St. James, Missouri.

Warrenton, Missouri.

Flat River, Missouri.

47

GREYHOUND
HALF-WAY HOUSE

Flat River, Missouri. Located along routes of Greyhound Lines for convenience and comfort of passengers.

Waterman's Cafeteria, Rolla, Missouri. Mr. and Mrs. Andy Waterman, owners and agent for Greyhound and M.K. & O. Bus Lines. Will seat 200 people. Can seat and feed 4 bus loads in 45 minutes. Open 24 hours a day.

Joplin, Missouri, Union Bus Terminal. The leading bus lines from Chicago, St. Louis, Kansas, and other points provide frequent services to and from the great southwest and the Ozarks.

Mueller's Dineateria, Van Horn, Texas. Your best stop on U.S. 80-90, Texas 54.

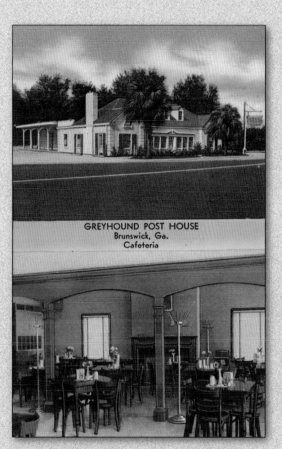

GreyhoundPostHouse,Brunswick,Georgia. Modern air conditioned Cafeteria. Located mid-way between Jacksonville, Florida and Savannah, Georgia on U.S. Route 17.

El Paso, Texas.

El Paso, Texas.

Sierra Blanca, Texas.

Ranger, Texas.

Greyhound Bus terminal and Greyhound Post House Cafeteria located in downtown Waco, Texas.

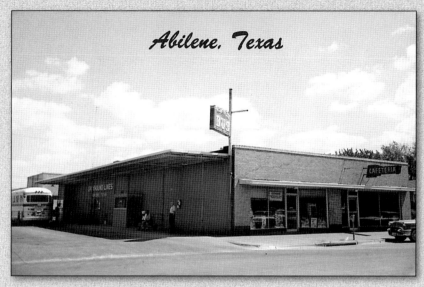

Greyhound Bus Station and Post House located in downtown Abilene, Texas. Abilene is well known as a transportation center.

Greyhound Post House, Pecos, Texas. This new and modern bus terminal, which has 26 schedules a day, and its fleet of fine buses is indeed a contrast to the vehicles that came through here in the days of Butterfield, Chisholm, and Goodnight-Loving Trails. Pecos (Indian for crooked—describing the Pecos River) was crossroads for those trails.

Greyhound Bus Terminal located at Lamar & Commerce, Dallas, Texas.

Laredo, Texas. The most important gateway to Mexico. Looking North on U.S. highway 81.

51

Howdy from Big Spring, Texas

Big Spring, Texas. Greyhound Bus Station and Post House Cafeteria with Hotel Settles in the background. Big Spring is a major transportation center with schedules to all points.

Greyhound Bus Depot. Bluebonnet Hotel in background. San Antonio, Texas.

Greyhound Bus Station and Post House in downtown Amarillo, Texas.

Greyhound Bus Terminal, North and Commerce Streets, Fort Worth, Texas. The spacious loading area is large enough to accommodate eighteen buses at once. Sixty-eight arrivals and departures daily making the terminal a hub of activity 24 hours a day.

Houston, Texas.

Atlanta, Georgia.

Kloesel's Resturant, Intersection Highways 90 & 77, Schulenburg, Texas. Come anytime! We are open 24 hours. Our restaurant is new, modern, and fully air-conditioned. Our food, it's delicious.

Terminal Cafeteria, Greyhound Bus Depot, Atlanta, Georgia. This cafeteria accommodates the 25,000 people who daily pass through the Atlanta Greyhound Bus Depot.

Cartersville, Georgia.

La Fayette, Georgia.

LaGrange, Georgia.

Greyhound Bus Station, McRae, Georgia. Excellent café.

Biloxi, Mississippi.

Cullman, Alabama.

Keener, Alabama.

Troy, Alabama.

Mobile, Alabama. Admiral Semmes Hotel and Bus Terminal, are both new and modern buildings facing Government Street which is a part of the old Spanish trail. Both buildings are located within two blocks of the entrance of Bankhead Tunnel, which passes under Mobile River.

Tuscaloosa, Alabama.

Flomaton Bus Station Café. U.S. 31 & 29, Flomaton, Alabama. "Where friends meet and the hungry eat." Texaco Gas & Oil—we never close.

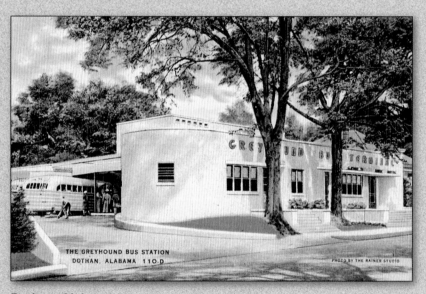

Dothan, Alabama.

Greetings from Birmingham, Alabama. The greyhound Bus Station provides many services for the traveler and parcel shipper. An outstanding Cafeteria and news stand are maintained by Greyhound Post Houses. Birmingham is "the youngest of the world's great cities."

Gulfport, Mississippi.

Jackson, Mississippi. Greyhound Lines Bus Depot, one of the most up-to-date depots in the entire Southland.

Jacksonville, Florida.

Greyhound Grill and Bus Station - Cordele, Ga. 2-U-339

Cordele, Georgia.

Greyhound Bus Station - Columbus, Ga. 2-0-89

Columbus, Georgia.

SCENE AT TAVERNIER, FLA. 5-200

Tavernier, Florida.

Bus Station - Marianna, Fla. 2-B-373

Marianna, Florida.

58

Greyhound, Florida.

Lake City, Florida.

Williston, Florida.

Yemasse, South Carolina.

Tallahassee, Florida.

Eustis, Florida. Bay St. near the crossing of Magnolia, one of the attractive thoroughfares lined with waving palms. The ACL Railway Station and the Greyhound Bus Stop in the foreground on the left.

Stephen Foster Restaurant. At the Suwannee River, on Route 98-27 & 19 at Fannin Springs, Florida. Famous for Suwannee River catfish & hushpuppies. Open 24 hours daily. Owned and operated by Mr. & Mrs. G. K. Page.

Greyhound Bus Station. U.S. No 1. Fort Pierce, Florida. 3,300 square feet of floor space with Rest Rooms, Waiting rooms, and Restaurant which serves the best food 24 hours a day. Mr. and Mrs. R. W. Nelson owners.

Greyhound Terminal and Post Cafeteria. 138 So. Ridgewood Ave, Daytona Beach, Florida.

Homestead, Florida. The Greyhound Scenicruiser, now serving passengers from New York to Miami. Completely air-conditioned, accommodates 33 passengers on raised rear level, and 10 passengers in forward section. Modern, complete washroom, and huge picture window for all passengers. Greyhound's most modern luxury bus.

Memphis, Tennessee.

Gaffney, South Carolina.

61

GREYHOUND BUS DEPOT. SPARTANBURG. S. C.

Spartanburg, South Carolina.

GREYHOUND BUS STATION - SELMER, TENN.

Feb. 12

Selmer, Tennessee.

Bus Station - Athens, Tenn. Y-46

Athens, Tennessee.

Athens Bus Station Cafe
Athens, Tenn.

Y-44

Athens, Tennessee.

La Follette, Tennessee.

Helenwood, Tennessee.

Monteagle, Tennessee.

Jackson, Tennessee.

Jackson, Tennessee.

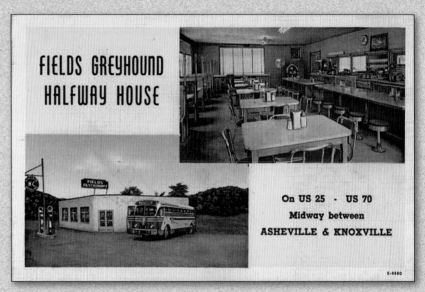

Del Rio, Tennessee. Fields Greyhound Halfway House. H. A. Fields, Prop. Specializing in country ham, fried chicken, and steaks. Never closed. On U.S. 25, U.S. 70. halfway between Asheville & Knoxville.

Lexington, Kentucky.

Lexington, Kentucky.

Paducah, Kentucky.

Norfolk, Virginia.

Falmouth, Virginia. Victor's Hollywood Restaurant. Fifteen acre camp with modern cabins. Greyhound rest stop. A good place to eat, specializing Italian spaghetti and Southern chicken dinners. No. 1 highway, 4 miles north of Fredericksburg. 45 miles South of Washington.

The Glass House Restaurant, South Hill, Virginia. Is unique, being built almost entirely of glass brick. The restaurant is operated by The Interstate Co. and is the outstanding eating-place on U.S. Highway no.1, between New York, and Miami.

Greyhound Inn Motel-Somerset, Kentucky. Air conditioned. Situated on Highway 27. Restaurant features home style cooking. Open 24 hours.

Somerset, Kentucky. The cafeteria is located next to the Greyhound Inn Motel in the foothills of the Cumberland Mountains, six miles from the scenic Cumberland Lake, the best fishing location in the state of Kentucky.

Greyhound Bus Terminal. Louisville, Kentucky.

Wytheville, Virginia.

Newport News, Virginia.

Gill's Grill and Grocery. U.S. Routes 58 & 15 in the heart of Clarkesville, Virginia. On beautiful "Bugg's Island Lake," boating, swimming, and fisherman's paradise. Sporting goods, Carolina boats, Johnson Motors. Boats and motors for rent. Live bait. Serving breakfast, lunch, and dinner. Specializing in pan-fried chicken, hot biscuits, and Maxwell House Coffee. Our coffee has made us famous. Open from 5 a.m. until midnight.

Gauley Bridge, West Virginia. Located where the Gauley and New River form the Great Kanawha.

Greyhound Bus Station, Huntington, West Virginia.

Charleston, West Virginia.

Wheeling, West Virginia.

Greyhound Post House. U.S. Route No. 40. Two miles south of Havre de Grace, Maryland. Frank Murphy, Manager.

Havre de Grace, Maryland.

Greyhound Bus Terminal, Baltimore, Md.

3B-H71

Baltimore, Maryland.

FOOD CAFETERIA

Clemente's Cafeteria, Official Greyhound Bus Stop, 166 S. DuPont Highway, New Castle, Delaware. Catering to chartered busses from Maine to Florida. Located halfway between New York and Washington.

GREYHOUND

BUS STATION, WINSTON-SALEM, N. C.

Winston-Salem, North Carolina, is a city of churches, schools and substantial business institutions where the home is paramount and where cooperation is the foundation of community life.

192—Greyhound Bus Terminal, Washington, D. C.

GREYHOUND

Arrived in Washington *Leaving for*

OB-H974

Washington D.C.

Oxford, Pennsylvania.

Bedford, Pennsylvania.

Bath, New York.

Bath, New York.

Greyhound Bus Terminal and Transporting Building, Philadelphia, Pennsylvania. Located between 17th and 18th on Market Street, and showing section of Penn Center and City Hall in background.

Greyhound Bus Depot, Main Street, Buffalo, New York.

Main Dining Room, Greyhound Post House, Boston, Massachusetts.

Pittsburgh, Pennsylvania. The beautiful new and modern Greyhound Bus Station and Ramp Parking Garage.

71

838   Greyhound Bus Terminal, Pittsburgh, Pa.

GREYHOUND LINES

Pittsburgh, Pennsylvania.

GREYHOUND BUS TERMINAL AND RESTAURANT, SCRANTON, PA.

45365

Scranton, Pennsylvania.

81—Greyhound and West Ridge Bus Depot,
N. Perry Square, Erie, Pa.

GREYHOUND
WEST RIDGE
GREYHOUND

ZB-H1316

Erie, Pennsylvania.

CENTRAL GREYHOUND LINES BUS TERMINAL, MONTGOMERY AND HARRISON STREETS, SYRACUSE, N. Y.

GREYHOUND

E-539B

Syracuse, New York.

Everett, Pennsylvania.

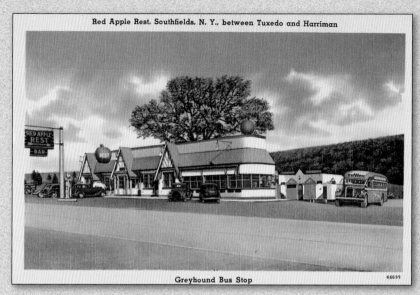

Southfields, New York.

Bridgeville, New Jersey.

Stewartstown, Maryland.

Galeton, Pennsylvania.

Greyhound Post House, Boston Post Road, Green Farms, Connecticut. Greyhound Rest Stop with complete facilities.

Albany, New York. The Greyhound Bus Terminal.

Canton, New York.

Port Allegany, Pennsylvania. Travel point since pioneer days, when travelers coming overland from the Susquehanna continued by water from "Canoe Place." The town grew as a center of lumber and tanning industry. Its descriptive present name came into use about 1840.

Dining Room Greyhound Post House. State College, Pennsylvania. "Home of the Pennsylvania State College."

Brockport, New York.

Canada

Bud's Coffee Shop and Dining Room. Bassano, Alberta. 4 miles from the famous Bassano Dam. Midway between Calgary and Medicine Hat on the Trans-Canada Highway. Stop for a snack and enjoy the food that is "the best in the west by a Dam site."

Greyhound Bus Depot and Prince Charles Hotel. Penticton, British Columbia.

Greyhound Bus Depot and Voyageur Restaurant. Swift Current, Saskatchewan. Your hosts: Irene & Norm Hunter. Our pledge: Good food with prompt courteous service.

Winnipeg Bus Terminal, Winnipeg, Manitoba. Located conveniently next door to the functional new bus depot, Rypp's Pharmacy is itself the last word in what modern, spacious and warm drug store ought to be. Bright, modern lighting enhances the wide varied displays of merchandise. Shopping convenience and economy are the biggest guidelines.

Blenheim, Ontario

Up-to-date shopping facilities await the visitors to Kenora, Ontario, Canada, on a beautiful Lake of the Woods.

Wainfleet, Ontario.

Hotel Oasis, Cache Creek, British Columbia. A modern, completely air-conditioned 32-room Hotel and Coffee shop, at the Sportsman's Crossways-Junction of the Trans-Canada and Cariboo Highways.

STAGE TERMINAL, EDMONTON, ALBERTA.

Edmonton, Alberta.

MEDICINE HAT

Medicine Hat, Alberta.

Bus Depot, Princeton, B.C.,

J.C. WALKER

Princeton, British Columbia.

BUS STOP ON CRESCENT AVE. SOURIS, MAN.

V334

Souris, Manitoba.

More Great Titles From Iconografix

All Iconografix books are available from direct mail specialty book dealers and bookstores worldwide, or can be ordered from the publisher. For book trade and distribution information or to add your name to our mailing list and receive a **FREE CATALOG** contact:

Iconografix, Inc.
PO Box 446, Dept BK
Hudson, WI, 54016

Telephone: (715) 381-9755,
(800) 289-3504 (USA),
Fax: (715) 381-9756

*This product is sold under license from Mack Trucks, Inc. Mack is a registered Trademark of Mack Trucks, Inc. All rights reserved.

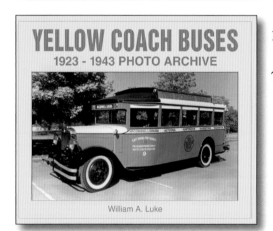

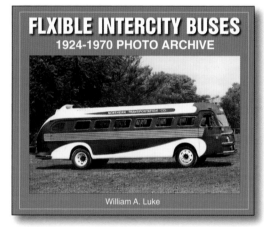
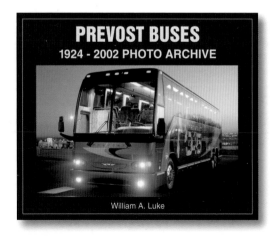
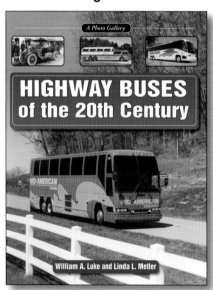
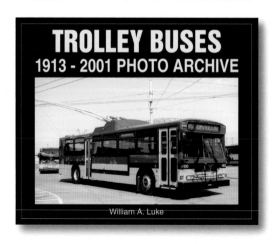